THE "ELECT LADY"
IN MINISTRY NOW

THE "ELECT LADY" IN MINISTRY NOW

Queen E.W. McCormick, D.Min.

XULON PRESS

Xulon Press
2301 Lucien Way #415
Maitland, FL 32751
407.339.4217
www.xulonpress.com

Unless otherwise indicated, Scripture quotations taken from The Amplified Bible, 1987; Dake's Annotated Reference Bible, 1991; Scofield Reference Bible; The Holy Scriptures according to the Masoretic Text, 1988.

Paperback ISBN-13: 978-1-5456-1809-7
eBook ISBN-13: 978-1-6628-2583-5

Dedicated in Memory of

Bishop Samuel Lee McCormick, husband

Reverend Minnie Lee Williams, mother

Bishop Solomon Williams, Sr., father

Elder Solomon Williams, Jr., brother

Mr. Joseph Williams, brother

Ms. Joann Williams, sister

Mrs. Margaret L. Porter, sister

Mrs. Rosa Williams Campbell, grandmother

Elder Rosa Lee Hardimon Thomas, pastor during early life

Bishop Designate, General Elder B.J. McCormick, father-in-law
and final pastor

Mrs. Pennie Lee McCormick, mother-in-law

Bishop M.F. L. Keith, chief overseer during early life

Bishop W.L. Nelson, Presiding State Bishop

Elder Levi Wilson, Presiding Elder

"Forever in our Hearts"
In Loving Memory

Senior Pastor Angela McCormick
November 12, 1962 – August 6, 2021

New Birth House of Prayer for All People, Inc.
Apostle Dr. Queen McCormick, Overseer

Acknowledgements

I owe many thanks to my late husband, Bishop Samuel McCormick; our daughters (Esther, Deborah, Angela, Julie, April, and Christine), nephew (Michael), and my deceased father, Bishop Solomon Williams, Sr., for their enduring cooperation and encouragement; to my deceased brother, Solomon Williams, Jr., who served as an elder and gave me my first reference Bible; to my entire family; to the officers and members of New Birth House of Prayer for All People, Inc., for their support and understanding; to all of my teachers, especially Mrs. Alzora Goodrum-Simmons, for their inspiration and encouragement throughout the years; to Bishop Frank Green, Bishop L.N. Quince, Jr.; Missionary Eunice Poole, Mother Grace Morman, Apostle Dr. Idell Cheevers, Prophet Brian Moseley, and Bishop Dr. Henry L. Porter for being my examples of faith; and to the Williams sisters for our accomplishments together in international music evangelism.

Special thanks go to Mrs. Lillie Brant, Miss Rana Bryant, Mrs. Verna J. Thomas, Mrs. Frances Meredith, and Mrs. Erica Mitchell for typing the original manuscript; to Ms. Edwena Smith for transcribing notes; to Dr. Mercy Moore for editing a portion of the manuscript; to Mrs. Clara Williams for editing and typing the third edition; to Mrs. Verna J. Michel for designing the original front cover; to Deborah McCormick Bailey, Julie McCormick and Dr. Yvette M. Giles for final edits to the most recently revised edition; and to all others who may have contributed to this work; to God, our Father and the Lord Jesus Christ, for inspiration; and to you, the readers of this book. May you be blessed with more understanding and revelational knowledge.

Table of Contents

Part Two: Elect Ladies in the Bible

Preface

$\mathcal{W}$ hen I originally wrote the words in this book, the concept of the "elect lady" was one not often examined in houses of worship. It was not until perhaps the late 1990s that the advanced and escalating roles of women in various areas of ministry were recognized. This recognition came through organizational heads, denominational conferences and associations, as it became clear that women were being used by God. In abundant numbers, elect ladies have been called into the pastorate. Additionally, some have been called to be apostles, prophets, evangelists, or teachers (Ephesians 4:11). Traditional teachings that promoted women keeping silent in the sanctuary have submitted their understanding to the Holy Spirit and a clarion release of elect ladies has been evident.

How do women like me and those who are engaging in this work know that they are elect ladies? We must first understand that when we accept salvation, we are already chosen. In that moment of salvation, we become part of the chosen generation. Within the "chosen generation, the royal priesthood, the holy nation, and the peculiar people" (1 Peter 2:9) are those whom God chooses for a specific assignment solely for Him. This foundational understanding of what it is to be a person of elect status, an elect lady, is the reason the Word of God exhorts us to "give diligence to make your calling and election sure" (2 Peter 1:10). To be an elect lady means you are being called out and separated from to fulfill a defined mission under the direct guidance and supervision of the Father.

We must also understand that even in the selection, in the calling out, all elect ladies are not called to be apostles like me (God has given apostleship); nor are called prophets, evangelists, pastors or teachers. Elect ladies who will not walk in these impartation ministries are called to the ministry of helps (1 Cor. 12:28). These elect ladies are purposely designed and trained by the Holy Spirit to help advance the kingdom in many ways. Consequently, we understand that the election of a lady for God's purpose is divinely ordained in each instance. For example, the elect lady may have the election to serve as a wife such as in the case of Sarah to Abraham. She may also serve as a mother, sister, mid wife, or patroness used to preserve the life of Moses for God's purpose. Whatever her election is, she must commit to it understanding that her election is pertinent to the ministry of those in the Kingdom. Her election is additionally as pertinent for those to whom we are to go into the highways and byways and feed the gospel.

My dear elect ladies do not miss the important understanding that separation is a vital component of your election, "separated but not segregated". In my election, I was separated from a church in which I had been nurtured and with which I longed to be. The church had been a part of our family and our lives for forty years. I had to leave my parents and my siblings. I loved that church, and I did not want to go. In leaving this church, I was also separated from ministering through music with the choirs and my precious sisters. But God spoke to me and said, "You either stay here and disobey Me, or you come out and do what I've called you to do."

While my husband supported me in the building of ministry in the home and in places of worship through the years, we were additionally separated. Our marriage did not falter as God's purpose in my election manifested, yet for quite some time we went separate ways in the paths of ministry in which we traveled for 22 years until God caused a great change.

Ministry, even for an elect lady, must always be present in the home and in the family. I share in this body of work that my daughters were reared participating in the work of the Lord. It was the way I was nurtured. The evidence and presence of ministry in our family allowed God's vision to manifest not only through me, but through my husband and our daughters. There have been times during the forty- plus years of serving in the pastorate that his (my husband's vision) moved us into larger facilities to gather God's sheep and to oversee the outreach churches of the ministry. This level of covering and support stayed with me until the Lord gave my husband eternal rest in 2010. Accepting your calling as an elect lady must come with and be bathed in humility, for it is the Lord who knows fully why you were elected. You must believe the Lord wholeheartedly and trust His Word. You must accept and believe the Holy Ghost as your guide and the One who imparts the gifts and callings that we are to have in the body of Christ. This is true whether you are female or male. God is not concerned with your sex. He is concerned with your commitment to Him and what He calls you to do. He is not concerned with color, culture, or nationalities; He is concerned with our spirits. When we are born again, we receive the Spirit of God that anoints us for specific duties, ministries, and times that God has for each of us.

When you acknowledge and then transition into your election, understand that even those closest to you may not be certain of your calling. When I moved into obedience, my parents, my former pastor, and my husband really did not understand it – they simply watched me. Ultimately, my husband fully accepted the election, and his faith in what God was doing in my life became a blessing. If you know that He called you to be an apostle, prophet, evangelist, pastor or teacher – be it and move forward. Your sure election comes through the fervent and passionate study of the Word of God and revelation through the Holy Spirit. Be sure that your election lines up with the Word; become one with the Father, and with the Word allow the Holy Spirit to manifest your election. Your instruction will come through revelation knowledge, and the knowledge will be confirmed as God so ordains.

Keep your eyes on the Lord and shut off the opposition. Opposition is evident in every election. We see this in our country and abroad in natural politics and even the body of Christ. Your responsibility is to the revelation, the election and the ordination – not to the opposition. I have tried to prove in several instances through the years that God called me. But my dear elect ladies, let go of that urging to correct those who oppose. Instead, just be inspired by how Jesus handled those who opposed Him. He would tell them, and so you can relay the same – I am not alone, my Father is with me. Whatever He says to speak, I speak; whatever He says to do, I do. This opposition will come from males and females, those in your denomination; some you call family and others are friends.

Finally, be obedient to your election. Do not harden your heart and close your ears to the urging and clarion call of God the Father. Your election may not be acknowledged nor promoted by your place of worship. Remember, Jesus said you are not alone. Hearken to the voice of the Holy Spirit, and when He says move, go, plant, feed, serve here or there–respond in obedience to the Father. God has given us the power and inner glory to carry out His divine appointment. We must rest in His humble spirit and allow that glory to pull us forward into our election.

Gaining Understanding

$\mathcal{W}$isdom is the principal thing; therefore get wisdom; and with all thy getting get understanding (Proverbs 4:7).

It is my intention of this study, therefore:

1. To instill understanding and dispel doubt and ignorance regarding women in ministry – women who have been elected by God to serve in any capacity for the cause of physical or spiritual salvation, whether as helpers or leaders;

2. To promote wider acceptance of women in ministry;

3. To encourage aspiring females who sense the call of God to ministry to yield to Him in service in every place where He calls. Through women in the ministry yielding to Christ, unbelievers may be converted, and saints be preserved in Him until the day of His coming, thus glorifying His name.

To lend support for greater understanding, a <u>definition of ministry</u> is included in the writing of this book, along with a statement of <u>purpose of election</u> and two summaries of the <u>doctrine of election</u> by two noted Bible scholars, C.I. Scofield and Fenis Jennings Dake. In addition are four scholarly opinions of Amplified Bible, Dake's Annotated Reference Bible, Eerdman's Concise Bible Handbook, and Scofield Reference Bible along with my interpretation in that order, let us begin with the word ministry.

Ministry

he New Strong's Exhaustive Concordance of the Bible references "ministry" more than twenty times with five different applications: three in Hebrew (Shareth, Abodah, Yad) and two in Greek (Diakonia, Litourgeo). In both Hebrew and Greek, the applications, in general, refer to service in the temple; minister, ministry, work of any kind (secular or sacred); aid; and relief.

The theme of this book was developed from the standpoint of the definition, work of any kind. Even though the biblical characters presented in this book were not all Jewish and were not all Jehovah worshippers, all of them were divinely influenced by Him. Otherwise, salvation could not have been achieved in the life of Moses, nor in the preservation of the nation of Israel, God's chosen people, in their fight to conquer Jericho. In both instances, He proved that He was Master and that salvation belonged to Him (Psalm 3:8).

Purpose of Election

To everything there is a season, and a time for every purpose under the heaven: a time to be born, and a time to die... (Ecclesiastes 3:1-2). And we know that all things work together for good to those who love God, to them who are called according to his purpose (Romans 8:28). In Greek, the word "purpose" suggests a deliberate plan, a proposition; an intention, or a design (Hayford).

God is at work to cause events to ultimately conclude for the good of His people, and often He uses us, His people, as agents in that process. We are, at those times, part of His advanced plan, fulfilling His purpose through our lives (Hayford).

To fulfill His *purpose* through us, God uses the process of election. For example, when the time had come for furtherance of the promise made by God to Abraham, God selected Jacob, the younger son of Isaac, to be the recipient of the birthright instead of Esau, the elder — an act contrary to Jewish tradition. Ordinarily, the birthright belonged to the firstborn (Dake). The scripture explains to that effect: *For the children being not yet born, neither having done any* good *or evil, that the purpose of God according to election might stand, not of works, but of*

Him that *calleth); it was said unto her, the elder shall serve the younger (Genesis 25:23; Romans 9:11-12).*

Doctrine of Election Summaries

 n the subject of election, Dake explains that there are four elects of God:

1. Christ
2. All Christians
3. Israel
4. Angels

Anyone chosen of God at any time, Jew or Gentile, is the "elect" of God. All men are called to become God's elect or chosen ones, and can be if they will choose God (Dake). However, it is my belief that in His sovereignty, "God makes exceptions as with Thermuthis, Pharaoh's daughter for the purpose of saving Moses."

Scofield adds that, in the testaments, Hebrew and Greek words such as "election," "choose" or "chosen" may also be used to signify the elect concept. In all cases, they mean, simply, *chosen* or *to choose* and are used for both human and divine choices.

1. In the latter use, election is

   a. corporate, as of the nation of Israel, or of the Church
   b. individual

2. Election is according to the foreknowledge of God and wholly by grace, apart from human merit, and

3. Election proceeds from the divine volition.

Election is, therefore

1. The sovereign act of God in grace, whereby certain persons are chosen from among mankind for Himself and

2. The sovereign act of God, whereby certain elect persons are chosen for distinctive service for HIM (Scofield).

General Statement

In light of the foregoing statements about <u>ministry, purpose of election and doctrine of election</u>, we will view, in the Old and New Testaments, a group of females chosen by God to perform distinctive service for Him or serve in a ministry vocation vital to His plan of redemption and essential to furthering Christianity as the Lord worked through them.

But first, in chapter 1, the Elect Lady of the 2 Epistle of John is defined; followed by the Personal Ministry Experience and Observation of the author, etc.... as noted in the order of part one in the table of contents.

Part two proceeds with Elected Ladies as Faith Sheroes. In the first scenario taken from the Old Testament, God chose Sarai/Sarah to be a mother of nations. Many Kings including the King of Kings – Christ Jesus came through her (Genesis 17:15-16).

The second scenario also taken from the Old Testament, five ladies (Jochebed who was Moses' mother; Miriam, the sister of Moses: Shiphrah and Puah were the midwives who disobeyed Pharoah's proclamation to kill all male babies; and Thermutis, Pharoah's daughter) all were chosen by God for the purpose of saving the life of baby Moses, the future leader of the Israelites, from destruction at a time when all males were threatened to be killed at birth.

The next scenario shows a Gentile harlot who was actively involved in helping the Israelites conquer her city, Jericho, an act of treason that resulted in salvation for her and her family.

Subsequently, in the New Testament, the curtain opens on the lives of several prominent women in Jesus' life. Elizabeth was barren and advance in years, yet God chose her to carry John the Baptist – who was the forerunner of Jesus Christ. God chose the virgin Mary to carry Jesus Christ the Messiah. Anna, a widowed prophetess was one of the two witnesses who gave thanks to God and spoke of the arrival of Christ the Messiah to the world. The Samaritan woman at the well was used to spread the word about salvation to other Samaritans. Other pertinent females include Priscilla, Junia and the elect lady, who were in ministry, a calling unique to women in the early Christian church. We will discuss the elect lady as defined in chapter 1.

PART ONE

JOURNEY OF APOSTLE DR. QUEEN E. MCCORMICK– AS AN ELECT LADY OF GOD

The Elect Lady Defined: Understandings by the Author, the Word of God and Bible Scholars 2 John 1:1-13

*Let everyone be fully convinced (satisfied) in his own mind (**Amplified Bible**, Romans 14:5)*

AUTHOR'S OPINION

*T*HIS IS MY OPINION ABOUT "THE ELECT LADY and her children," described in the Second Epistle of John. My persuasion is derived from two specifics of the letter. The first is in the salutation: "the elder unto the elect lady and her children" (Verse 1); and the second is within the body: "and now I beseech thee lady ..." (Verse 5). Astounding! Impressive and notable is the elect lady. She is the first and only female addressed by an Apostle in all of the 22 Epistles. From these two verses, development of the theme is pursued, so as to show that there is true equality in Christ Jesus for females, not only in worship but also in ministry leadership. Thus "the elect lady" is depicted here as the pastor and "her children," the fruit of her labor, the local church that possibly met in her home.

Be it known, also, that there is not male or female in Christ Jesus, nor respect of persons to those who are born again; for this reason, neither nationality, sex, nor status in life matters. So then, "the elect lady" could have been a single, divorced, widowed, or married woman, with the privilege of her birthright, as a citizen of the Kingdom of God, to produce spiritual children. Bearing witness to that effect, the scripture informs believers that children of the Kingdom of God are not born of flesh and blood, or of the will of man, but of God. "Of His own will begat he us with the word of truth" (John 1:12-13; 1 Peter 1:23; James 1:18).

With those thoughts in mind, let us move forward to discuss the issue at hand. My theory concludes, as I believe, that the elect lady was a woman of great importance, who was chosen by God for special work. She was married and had children who, like her, were born again. They met with other Christians in her house, as they continued steadfastly in the apostles' doctrine: in fellowship, in breaking of bread, and in prayers (Acts 2:42). She, without doubt, was raised, qualified, and appointed by the Holy Ghost to have special care and oversight to "feed the flock" (Acts 20:17 & 28). This I speak by the authority of the Holy Ghost and from experience derived from obedience to Him who called me.

During the summer that the Lord called me into full-time ministry, He convinced me to read the Second Epistle of John. Fascinated by the salutation, "The elder unto the elect lady and her children," I continued to read. As I read, I saw some identification marks with which I could identify: the favor of God and our children. Realizing the similarity that existed, I thought on the words of Solomon in Ecclesiastes: "That which hath been is now; and that which is to be hath already been; and God requireth that which is past ... and there is no new thing under the sun" (Ecclesiastes 3:15; 1:9).

I thought again of Mary, the virgin, who was chosen by God to bear Jesus Christ the Messiah, His only begotten Son, and of her words of submission as she yielded to His call. Then I said as she said, "Behold, the handmaiden of the Lord; be it unto me according to thy word" (Luke 1:38). With that, I surrendered and thanked the Lord for counting me worthy to entrust the ministry of the Word into my hand.

As we continue with this discussion, it is important to note that Apostle Elder John addresses the lady as **elect**. She is mentioned first and then her children... (2 John 1:1). Observe also that she is the only person addressed in verse 5. "And I beseech thee lady..." This indicates that the lady is someone in authority who exercises influence over others and is someone with whom the apostle directly communicates the message of truth and love (verse 1-6), warning against deceivers and antichrists and giving precaution for backsliders and what to do in these instances (verses 7-11). To whom would she relate this message? To her children, of course. Whether by nature biologically or by the new birth is not stated, but the pronouns "her" and "thy" both show ownership and possession. They were her children! No ifs, ands, or buts about it; we cannot escape the fact that the children belonged to her, and she was their mother!

ELECT LADY'S CHILDREN DEFINED

Children in Greek implies child (as produced); daughter, son; to produce from seed as a mother (literally and figuratively); bear, be born, bring forth; be delivered; be in travail (Strong). In this sense, it is doubly possible that the elect lady produced from seed, as a mother, biological children, and on the other hand, she brought forth spiritual children into the kingdom by the seed, which is the Word of God preached (Luke 8:11).

After these children were born again, she cared for them. The duties she performed are known compactly as "mothering", which, according to the dictionary, means to give birth to; to be the mother to; to create and care for; to instigate and carry through; to watch over, nourish, and protect (*American Heritage Dictionary*). Even though the term "mothering" is not mentioned in the Bible, the term does describe the duties of a pastor.

According to Vines, the pastor is a shepherd, one who tends herds or flocks, and not merely one who feeds them... <u>Christian pastors</u> (Ephesians 4:11) guide as well as <u>feed</u> the flock, a service committed to <u>elders, overseers, and bishops</u> (Acts 20:28; Vines). Merrill reiterates that a pastor then is a **divinely given shepherd** to tend, feed, and protect God's sheep (Merrill). Thus "to tend" is to supervise or take charge of, or to care for. Protect is to guard, defend, or watch over And to feed is to nurture and rule. In a nutshell, these unified duties are analogously rendered mothering.

Mother, in Israel, was a title of respect (Vines). Perhaps a more famous mother in scripture is Deborah (Old Testament). Deborah, besides her duty as the wife of Lapidoth, was a prophetess and the only woman judge in Israel. In that position, she ruled, governed, and defended her people (Strong). During her reign, she encouraged General Barak to fight against Sisera, commander of the army of Jabin and a Canaanite king. In subjection, Barak said, "If you will go with me, then I will go; but if you will not go with me, then I will not go." And she said, "I will surely go with you" (Judges 4:8-9). The resulting victory ended twenty years of Canaanite oppression. After the battle was fought and the victory was won, Deborah and Barak praised God. The former says "I, Deborah, arose a **mother** in Israel" (Judges 5:7).

Parallel to the spiritual mother is the spiritual father, whose duties are similar. Figuratively speaking, mothering is altogether familiar to the Apostle Paul, who as a spiritual father, made it known with the statement: "Besides those things that are without, which cometh upon me daily, is the inescapable care of all the churches" (2 Corinthians 11:28). These churches, the flock of disciples, were often referred to as "my children," or as in his working relationship with Timothy and Titus, the younger elders, "my sons." Observe the following scriptures:

APOSTLE PAUL DESCRIBES HIS CHILDREN

1 Corinthians 4:15-17

15 For though ye have ten thousand instructors in Christ, yet have ye not many fathers: for in Christ Jesus I have begotten you through the gospel.

16 Wherefore I beseech you, be ye followers of me.

17 For this cause have I sent unto you Timotheus, who is my beloved son, and faithful in the Lord, who shall bring you into remembrance of my ways which be in Christ, as I teach everywhere in every church.

Galatians 4:19

19 My little children, of whom I travail in birth again until Christ be formed in you,

Titus 1:4

4 To Titus, mine own son after the common faith: Grace, mercy, and peace, from God the Father and the Lord Jesus Christ our Savior.

Philemon 1:10

10 I beseech thee for my son Onesimus, whom I have begotten in my bonds:

Furthermore, on the authority of the aforementioned scriptures and from the standpoint of the words, her children and the author's assertion of mother and mothering is the derivative assumption:

The elect lady was a spiritual mother in the same sense as Deborah was in Israel and as Paul was spiritual father to Timothy, Titus, and to the disciples of Galatia, Corinth, and elsewhere. The elect lady (more probable than not) did tend, protect, and feed her children as a mother walking in truth and leading them as a shepherd in love.

No, the elect lady was not called elder, overseer, bishop, pastor, shepherd, or mother, for that matter. But one thing is certain, she got the job done, and it was appreciated by the Apostle John who, in his loving epistle, stated, "I rejoiced greatly, that I found some of your children walking in truth." Like Deborah and Paul, who were spiritual parents and leaders, it could be said then that the **elect lady** arose a mother in the church, and in all probability, she was the pastor of the flock in the church that was her house.

2 John 1:1-13
- Gaining Its Meaning and Wisdom

...the Lord seeth not as man seeth; for man looketh on the outward appearance, but the Lord looketh on the heart (Dake, 1 Samuel 16:7)

These words were spoken by Samuel, the prophet of the Lord, who was given charge to select the second king of Israel. He was told to anoint one of the eight sons of Jesse, the Bethlehemite.

With the eldest son, Eliab, Samuel looked up on him said, "surely the LORD's anointed was before him." But the Lord replied, not so! Look not on his countenance or on the height of his stature; because I have refused him: for the LORD seeth not as man seeth; for man looketh on the outward appearance, but the LORD looketh on the heart. (1 Samuel 16:7) So God chose David, the youngest son, instead of Eliab.

The heart is the spirit of man, male and female (Genesis 1:26-27). It is that part of man with which God communicates. The Bible says, "God is a Spirit: and they that worship him must worship him in spirit and in truth (John 4:24)."

Since the grace of God has come in its fullness through Jesus Christ, the Messiah, all believers have access to God. We are then His "chosen generation, a royal priesthood, an holy nation, [and] a peculiar people" (1 Peter 2:9-10), among which was the **elect lady** in the Second Epistle of John. In the letter, she is exemplified as special and so are her children. Let us read 2 John 1:1-13.

2 John 1:1-13

1 The elder unto the elect lady and her children, whom I love in the truth; and not I only, but also all they that have known the truth;

2 For the truth's sake, which dwelleth in us, and shall be with us forever.

3 Grace be with you, mercy, and peace, from God the Father, and from the Lord Jesus Christ, the Son of the Father, in truth and love.

4 I rejoiced greatly that I found of thy children walking in truth, as we have received a commandment from the Father.

5 And now I beseech thee, lady, not as though I wrote a new commandment unto thee, but that which we had from the beginning, that we love one another.

6 And this is love, that we walk after his command-ments. This is the commandment, That, as ye have heard from the beginning, ye should walk in it.

7 For many deceivers are entered into the world, who confess not that Jesus Christ is come in the flesh. This is a deceiver and an antichrist.

8 Look to yourselves, that we lose not those things which we have wrought, but that we receive a full reward.

9 Whosoever transgresseth, and abideth not in the doc-trine of Christ, hath not God. He that abideth in the doctrine of Christ, he hath both the Father and the Son.

10 If there come any unto you, and bring not this doctrine, receive him not into your house, neither bid him God speed:

11 For he that biddeth him God speed is partaker of his evil deeds.

12 Having many things to write unto you, I would not write with paper and ink: but I trust to come unto you, and speak face to face, that our joy may be full.

13 The children of thy elect sister greet thee. Amen.

As quoted, this brief and informative letter addressed to a woman has aroused quite a stir of controversy among some Bible scholars: "Who or what is the elect lady and her children?" Some opinions have been excerpted from the Scofield, the Amplified, and the Dake's Annotated Reference Bible, and the Erdman's Concise Bible Handbook, and are included for discussion in the next segment entitled, "Scholarly Opinions." About this matter, as you may observe, each commentator differs somewhat in their beliefs as presented.

Scholarly Opinions

The Amplified Bible

The second letter of John is addressed to "the elect (chosen) lady (Cyria) and her children" may refer to an individual and her family, or possibly to a church.

Dake's Annotated Reference Bible

The Greek word, "Kuria," feminine of Kurlos, which means Lord, may signify lady, or some most excellent and honorable woman whom John addressed in the epistle. She likely had a church in her home. She was a married woman, for her children are also saluted. No husband is mentioned, so perhaps she was a widow who entertained many ministers and traveling evangelists in her home.

Eerdman's Concise Bible Handbook

The "lady" is most probably a local church, rather than an individual. The "children" would then be church members (as in 1 John), and the lady's "sister" would likely be John's own church.

Scofield Reference Bible

The second epistle of John has, on account of its salutation, occasioned much discussion. Some scholars assert that the words, "the elect lady," personify one of the first century churches; others assume they refer to some highly placed Christian matron the Apostle, with whom John was acquainted.

Chapter 2

Personal Ministry and Observations

I must work the works of him that sent me, while it is day. John 9:4

THE TURNING POINT IN MY LIFE BEGAN with a sequence of four visions occurring in July 1978. All appeared early in the morning about six o'clock, a few days apart from each other. Subsequently, more of these supernatural revelations occurred in the years that followed. In them, the Lord revealed by divine volition the role for me in His plan. These visions had an immense effect in my life and most powerfully influenced and persuaded my decision to accept the call of God into full-time ministry; for which cause, I am, therefore, "separated but not segregated."

Before these phenomenal insights, I had served in almost every area of helps in the ministry. This service has continued through high school, through marriage, and until this present hour. My primary ministry then was in gospel music evangelism. Prior activities included President of the Young Folks and Friends Union, State Sunday School Convention

Superintendent, National Youth Panelist (religious), Youth Sunday Service Coordinator, and ministries of in-home visitation, hospitals, prisons and broadcasts. I also managed to be a part-time volunteer in school and civic affairs.

At the time of the call, I was singing with my sisters (Frances, Mary, Lillie, Joanne, and Jackie). In the mid-1950s, we were organized by our mother as the *Original Williams Sisters of Fort Lauderdale, Florida*. With the assistance of our father, our first recording, "God is Good/Jesus I'll Never Forget," was done in 1977 on the Hort Sullivan Label.

Many ministry doors opened to us individually and as a group. We ministered, not only in our hometown and in other states of our country but also in the Bahamas.

Even though my husband and I were married for thirty-seven years at that time (Hallelujah!) we were both very busy, together we raised our children and a nephew we considered as our son.

As the clock wound down and the wheels of time turned, I was content and confident knowing that my husband was to become a minister. In my heart, I pledged to support him wholeheartedly when the time came. But before his acknowledgment, something strange happened to me. At age thirty-seven, God decided to call me first to the ministry.

He chose a unique way of getting my attention by communicating with me in visions. The Hebrew word for visions, "hazon," signifies a means of divine revelations and denotes a prophetic vision by which divine messages are communicated. In Greek, the word for vision is "horama," meaning "that which is seen." The prophetic vision was the foremost method of conveying His instructions during that period. However, this has not been the only way He has spoken to me.

I confess that in the beginning I was perplexed. Curiously, I went about seeking and asking various ministers, "How did God call you to the ministry? What did He say to you?"

Some answered, "The Lord said 'go'!" Others said, "The Lord said, 'Preach.' The Lord said, 'Teach.'" Not one of these answers satisfied my hunger for confirmation of this new thing happening to me. The answer came only when I knelt and prayed and meditated in the Word. I realized that this was supernaturally from God – a call to serve. Many are called, but few are chosen (Matthew 22:14).

John 16:13 (Scofield)

Howbeit when he, the spirit of truth, is come, he will guide you into all truth; for he shall not speak of himself; but whatsoever he shall hear, that shall he speak: and he will show you things to come.

Habakkuk 2:2-3
Presenting the Visions

...Write the vision, and make it plain upon (tablets), that he may run that readeth it. For the vision is yet for an appointed time, but at the end it shall speak, and not lie; though it tarry, wait for it, because it will surely come, it will not tarry.

Chapter 3

Making the Call and Election Sure

*Wherefore the rather, brethren, give diligence to make
your calling and election sure: for if ye do these things,
ye shall never fall: For so an entrance shall be ministered unto you abundantly into the everlasting kingdom
of our Lord and Saviour Jesus Christ* (2 Peter 1:10-11)

*...Write the vision, and make it plain upon tables, that
he may run that readeth it. For the vision is yet for an
appointed time, but at the end it shall speak, and not lie:
though it tarry, wait for it; because it will surely come,
it will not tarry* (Habakkuk 2:2-3)

PRESENTING THE VISION

ONE BY ONE, THE PROPHETIC VISIONS CAME.
Startling, concise, written, and pictorial, they were so
impressive and presented in such a manner intended, I believe,
never to be forgotten by the beholder. Oh, the wonderful works
of God! I can picture them now as vividly as I saw them in
1978. That's just like God; He paints eternal pictures!

On the first day of July, in the summer of 1978, the Word of the Lord appeared to me, typewritten in bold black letters on a white background, saying, "I must work the works of Him that sent me, while it is day; the night cometh, when no man can work" (John 9:4).

An urgent, awesome feeling overcame me. Overtaken, I sat upright in bed, pondering in astonishment. Even though I felt compelled, I was not convinced because I did not fully understand. I began to read and pray every day, sometimes with fasting. Gradually, understanding unfolded. The testimony of Jesus in John's gospel helped tremendously.

"Verily, verily I say unto you, He that believeth on me the works that I do, shall he do also; and greater works than these shall he do, because I go to my Father" (John 14:12).

However, I was still stuck somewhat on the word "He" in that statement, because I am not a man; I am a woman. It was not until I read later the Epistle to the Galatians by the Apostle Paul that the light bulb in my mind flickered. The flickering got brighter as I read, "For in Christ Jesus, you are all sons of God through faith (*The Amplified Bible*; Galatians 3:26). "Sons," I thought, "That includes me." Then I thought again of the song I heard the primary class of our church sing, "Father Abraham has many sons, and many sons has Father Abraham; and I am one of them and so are you" (Author Unknown).

Further illuminations came as I continued to read. "For as many {of you} as were baptized into Christ {into a spiritual union and communion with Christ, the Anointed One, the Messiah} have put on (clothed yourselves with) Christ. There is {now no distinction} neither Jew nor Greek, there is neither slave nor free, there is not male and female; for you are all one in Christ Jesus. And if you belong to Christ {are in Him Who is Abraham's Seed}, then you are Abraham's offspring, and (spiritual) heirs according to promise" (*The Amplified Bible*, Galatians 3:27-29).

Additionally, further support was found in the following scripture.

John 1:12-13

12 But as many as received him, to them gave he power to become the sons of God, even to them that believe on his name:

13 Which were born, not of blood, nor of the will of the flesh, nor of the will ofman, but of God.

I perceived then that God is no respecter of persons. Not only am I the natural seed, born of flesh and blood, the offspring and daughter of Solomon and Minnie Lee Williams, but I am also born of the Spirit of God. I have a spiritual birthright that gives me access to the royal priesthood (The Amplified Bible, 1 Peter 2:9-10) "You are a chosen race, a royal priesthood, a dedicated nation, (God's) own purchased special people, that you may set forth the wonderful deeds and display the virtues and perfections of Him Who called you out of darkness into His marvelous light" (Exodus 19:5-6). "Once you were not a people {at all}, but now you are God's people; once you were unpitied, but now you are pitied and have received mercy" (Hosea 2:23; 1 Peter 2:10).

"Royal" in Greek is "basileios," meaning a king or belonging to a king; of the priesthood consisting of all believers (Vines, p. 978). Having been convinced that I am a son and a believer priest, I have decided that I must work the works of Him who sent me, while it is day.

In the next vision, I beheld the setting of a big crowd gathered in a huge auditorium. Therein, I could see my sisters and me as we stood in ministry formation, horizontally, side by side: Mary, Lillie, Frances, Jackie, and me. Joanne, my other sister who sang with the group, was ill at the time. Something unusual happened. Suddenly, with the microphone in my hand, I walked forward away from my sisters. Taking the lead, I began to proclaim in a loud voice, "Blessed are the poor in spirit for theirs is the kingdom of heaven. Blessed are they who do hunger and thirst after righteousness for they shall be filled." This vision was exceptional. Ordinarily, I sang background and, occasionally, second lead (Mary always started the songs).

At the conclusion of the dream, I awakened and hastily went into the living room and dining area, where my husband, Sam, and the rest of the family were occupied. As I stood by my husband sitting in the chair, I exclaimed excitedly, "Hey Y'all, I was preaching! At least, I was expounding the word of the Lord in a high-pitched voice." To this, my daughter Debbie later replied, "A preacher for a momma!"

Moving toward the end of the month, the Spirit revealed still another supernatural sight, which was the third vision. The object presented was a small white envelope with three black numbers mysteriously inscribed like this: "6:19." Afterward, I discussed the matter with Jackie, my sister. She thought, as I did, that these numbers might have been scripture references. So, from Genesis to Revelation, I searched and found only three books in the New Testament with six chapters that had a message at verse nineteen: Matthew, Romans and 1 Corinthians.

The first of these three apparitions was Matthew 6:19-21. Jesus said, "Lay not up for yourselves treasures upon earth, where moth and rust doth corrupt, and where thieves break through and steal. But lay up for yourselves treasures in heaven, where neither moth nor rust corrupt, and where thieves do not break through nor steal; For where your treasure is, there will your heart be also."

In Roman 6:19, the Apostle Paul exhorts the saints at Rome from a practical standpoint with a spiritual connotation: "I speak after the manner of men because of the infirmity in your flesh; for as you have yielded your members servants to uncleanness and iniquity, unto iniquity; even so now yield your members servants to righteousness, unto holiness." Finally, in 1 Corinthians 6:19, Paul asked believers a question: "What? Know ye not that your body is the temple of the (Holy Spirit) who is in you, whom ye have of God and you are not your own?"

Then he explains in verse 20, "For you are bought with a price; therefore, glorify God in your body and in your spirit, which are God's."

The unmasking of these revelations, brought on by reading the three directives, opened my eyes. Then I realized that I am not the owner of my life, God is. He is the potter and I am the clay. I became more willing than ever to submit to the course that He had chosen for my life and to proclaim, "I am yours, Lord, everything I am, everything I am not, everything I've got" (author unknown). By the end of July, while my sisters, daddy and I were on tour singing in the southern states of South Carolina, Alabama, and Louisiana, the last of the visions occurred as I lay asleep in a hotel bed in Camden, South Carolina. It was about six o'clock in the morning. Unlike the context of the three former visions, this was much different. It had a two- fold segment in which I plainly saw myself in the presence of a bedridden lady, apparently in a comatose state, having the appearance of one who is lifeless, lying on what appeared to be a hospital bed. Before I left, she was revived. Then the Spirit took me immediately into the presence of a fatherless little girl, whom I consoled. When the trance ended,

I awakened in amazement at what my eyes had beheld in the late 1970s – again, visions from the Lord.

CHAPTER 4

After the Silent Period

*Being confident of this very thing that he which hath
begun a good work in you will perform it until the day
of Jesus Christ...Philippians 1:6*

A YEAR-AND-A-HALF OF SILENCE PASSED
after the visions of July 1978. Breaking the silence
on January 3, 1980, with the first of four more visions, the Lord
proclaimed, "Out of Egypt I call my son."

The Spirit reminded me then of two sons: Israel as a nation
and Jesus as the greater son, who were both called out of Egypt
for a special purpose – to serve in the place He chose. Just as
they were called out of Egypt, so was I. We have been called
out of the world and translated into the kingdom of His dear
Son (Colossians 1:13).

On the next day, Friday, January 4th, He commanded,
"Plant four months." On Saturday, January 5th, He showed me
a vision of aggression that took place in my mouth. Plainly, I
saw my tongue assertively push the lower molar on the right

side until it was uprooted. Amazingly, there was no feeling of physical pain, but I experienced sorrow, mental anguish and an anti-social attitude. Then I wondered why one missing tooth caused so much grief when other individuals, who had no teeth at all, were happily going about and doing their regular activities. At that instant I decided, "In the name of Jesus, I've got commitments to keep." So, I got up and proceeded to where my husband was to tell him, but I awakened in a very sad mood, crying real tears. Finally, on Sunday, January 6, 1980 the last of these visions occurred saying, "The spirit of the Lord is upon me." In contrast to the day before, I awakened in a very joyful mood!

As this quartet of visions unfolded day by day, I sought comprehension. Even though my primary source of research was the Bible, I also sought help from my diocese bishop and presiding elder about two of these revelations. I wrote the bishop, but I received no response. When I saw him some time later, I inquired about the letter I sent. "I never received it," he said.

By that time, I had found the illumination that I needed about "Out of Egypt I call my son."

When I called the presiding elder about the second vision, ("Plant four months") he said, "Sounds to me like work." Then he instructed me to preach a lot about repentance.

On Thanksgiving Day of the same year, my husband and I were in Waycross, Georgia, attending a state assembly. That morning, I had next to the final vision of the year. This was the vision: As I walked up to the front of the church, I shook the hand of a lady I knew very well. She was standing by a table near the pulpit, in the praise leader's position. As I shook her hand, she started <u>laughing like a hyena</u>! I don't know why she was laughing, so I walked to the left side of the church where my father-in-law and pastor, Bishop Designate, General

Presiding Elder B.J. McCormick (now deceased) was sitting. I sat beside him and said, "Big Daddy, I am going to try to come back." Then I walked out the back door. Only God knew then why I said what I said and left.

Finally, on December 12, 1980, the Spirit alerted me, saying, "Something is going to happen in April." Fearing the worst (as the thought occurred over and over in my mind during the next few months), eventually I said in February 1981, "Lord, whatever it is, prepare me for it." Then I decided to devote myself to praying, fasting, and reading the Bible more intensely. On the forty-second day of consecration, which was April 1, something did happen. Contrary to what I had expected, the Holy Spirit calmly uttered, "New Birth." In that instant, the anxiety I felt disappeared. I was relieved, but mystified.

Later, in April, He manifested Himself to me twice and gave two commands in this order: "Feed the Flock!" and "Assemble all My people!" At the time these words were spoken, a little flock already existed. It had come into existence sixteen months earlier.

In January 1980, when He proclaimed and commanded respectively, "Out of Egypt I call my son!" and "plant four months," I immediately endeavored to obey, as I understood, and planted a garden of vegetables (collards, turnips, and cabbage) in our back yard. I hid the Word in my heart and held Bible study in our home with family and friends. Having considered these commands, there was no doubt in my mind that the Lord had called me to a special ministry to this flock and to all that He willed. My ministry, as a pastor, was born and so was New Birth House of Prayer for All People. Neger Ben Thomas, our neighbor was the first convert to get saved.

So that I would be more enlightened and encouraged to perform the last charge, "Assemble all my people," the Holy

Spirit brought to my remembrance the advice given to Pastor Timothy when he was left in charge of the church at Ephesus. The Apostle Paul admonished him in 2 Timothy 4:2-5, "Preach the word; be instant in season, out of season, reprove, rebuke, exhort with all longsuffering and doctrine . . . ; do the work of an evangelist and make full proof of thy ministry." These instructions line up with the great commission of our Lord, the Messiah, Christ Jesus, to His followers, "Go ye therefore into all the world, and preach the gospel to every creature. He that believeth and is baptized shall be saved, but he that believeth not shall be damned" (Mark 16:15-20; Matt. 28:19-20).

For that cause, I want to work alongside a collection of churches and denominations across the globe to fulfill my God-given task for reaching all of God's people with the message of salvation...

In November 2010, I heard the Lord say, "This year, I'm going to pour out my spirit through this woman and she shall preach, and signs shall follow. And when she speaks, I will confirm my word with signs and wonders." Since then, the Lord has taken me to other nations.

CHAPTER 5

Abiding in the Ministry of My Calling after Recognizing the Calling

AFTER MOVING FORWARD TO DO GOD'S WILL, AS REVEALED TO ME, I encountered great antagonism, strong reprimand, opposing confrontations and rejection. As evangelist pastor, the greatest act of hostility came across the radio waves from male counterparts, who openly reviled female pastors, and also from others.

I recall quite vividly my first one-on-one encounter with a man with whom I had a verbal confrontation. While we both waited for our automobiles to be serviced, he stood on my right side, and we amiably chatted. Suddenly, a remarkable change occurred when he learned of my position as a pastor. His facial demeanor appeared to become menacing. Vehemently, he pursed his lips, with his brow furled, he looked at me with fiery red beastly eyes. He said, in a voice raging with displeasure, "God didn't tell no woman to preach!"

Another time a lady accosted me in a restaurant. She, too, resented my ministry, using the identical words of the man aforementioned.

Later, a very close male relative said, "Your place is in the home, keeping the house. You ought to let Sam run the church and do more of the preaching."

Sometime later, a neighboring male member, whose church is on the same street as ours, saw my husband renovating our first church building, preparing for our first service. Trying to be friendly he asked, "Are you the pastor?"

When my husband replied, "No, my wife is," he said, "You should be the pastor."

Ironically, all of these sentiments were expressed by professed Christians of different denominations in the body of Christ. The ultimate aim of such oppositional forces was designed by the archenemy, Satan, to instill fear in me. But the Holy Spirit, my helper, and counselor present all the time, reminded me that "God hath not given us a spirit of fear" (2 Timothy 1:7). Prior to that, He had given a direct rhema warning. "Fear will cause you to miss heaven and go to hell." I felt awful when I heard Him say that, because the Bible says, "The fearful...shall have their part in the lake that burns with fire and brimstone, which is the second death" (Revelation 21:8). As Christians, we are exhorted to "Fear not them who kill the body, but are not able to kill the soul; but rather fear him, who is able to destroy both soul and body in hell." (Matthew 10:28). Jesus added in (Revelation 21:8) "But the fearful and unbelieving, and the abominable, and murderers, and whoremongers, and sorcerers, and idolaters, and all liars, shall have their part in the lake which burneth with fire and brimstone: which is the second death."

There were times, as a girl and even as an adult, when I allowed fear to rule my emotions, and the Lord brought two of these experiences back to my attention. First, He said, "Remember when you were a little girl and the neighborhood man gave all the children candy, and you didn't get any. Why? Because you were afraid of him."

"Remember when you were eight or nine years old, attending a youth convention, and you volunteered to sing your first solo? Suddenly, you began to cry and walked back to your seat. What happened? You didn't sing. Why? Because you were afraid." In these two instances, I allowed fear to rob me. I have come to realize over the years that fear hinders progress, healing and achievement. God wants us to prosper, but Satan does not. Satan's commission is to steal, kill, and destroy. Fear definitely is an enemy to us. It wars against the soul and prevents the reward of blessings and success. Thank God, I have overcome fear!

CHAPTER 6

Summarizing the Call and Election

ARLIER, I SHARED WITH YOU THE VISIONS, THE COMMANDS and other means by which God convinced me that I was His elect lady, chosen for distinctive service –walking in the roles of apostle, prophet, evangelist, pastor, and teacher – by appointment in this hour, but not all at the same time. I also shared with you how I searched the scripture day and night, weeks at a time, for verification according to 1 John 4:1, "test the spirits to determine whether they were of God through the Word of God," to make my calling and election sure. When I ascertained that He had given me the ministry of a pastor, I was grateful to know that He had chosen me to <u>guide, feed, tend, and exercise oversight</u> of the flock that required tender care and vigilant superintendence, a service committed to elders, overseers and bishops (Vines). Like Paul, I was not disobedient to the heavenly vision (Acts 26:19).

Concurring with the foregoing statements and from past experience as I ministered to <u>the church in our house</u> during the former years of ministry, I realize that the words of Dr. Charles Travis are true: "The Pastor is the most intimate with the flock of God; the shepherd of His sheep" (Travis). This apparently evolved from nearly two decades at that time of mothering the flock in regular fellowship that included over 1,644 Sunday meetings, not including weekly Bible study, such as crusades, baptisms, weddings, funerals and counseling sessions.

Furthermore, I received a greater awareness of the min-istry of helps, when the Lord "separated" me unto Himself (the gospel of God). As Priscilla and Aquila were beneficial to Paul as his helpers, God sent two prophetesses (E. Dorsett and G. Mormon) to encourage me to obey Him at the inaugura-tion of this ministry. Through the word of wisdom, knowledge, and discernment, I was edified and stabilized more in the faith and encouraged to walk in my new ministry (as an apostle) to "set up and move on". However, when the ministry was set up, He chose me to be the overseer (pastor) to "Feed the flock." I thank God that the prophetesses were my helpers, as Priscilla and Aquila were to Paul his helpers.

On the other hand, God used me in the same capacity in the body of Christ. A particular instance was made clear when I was speaking in Indiana as an invited minister. He said to me then, "You are a helper to this Pentecostal Bishop (N. Manning) and congregation now. As you are teaching, you are walking in both the ministry of helps and in the ministry of the teacher, thereby, edifying while embracing the **apostleship**."

In the early 1980's, for more than forty-five years at that time, I have walked with the Lord as a disciple, helper, and apostle in the five-fold ministry, as the Lord willed. As I have served, I am most confident with these words, that "He which hath begun a good work in you will perform it until the day of Jesus Christ." (Philippians 1:6)

Thank You, Father, for making my calling and election sure; for it was Your dwelling within me and You who were doing the work, while reminding me that "without Me, you can do nothing." (John 15:5)

> *"Verily Verily, I say unto you, He that believeth on me, the works that I do shall he do also; and greater works than these shall he do; because I go unto my Father."* (John 14:12)

CHAPTER 7

Church in the House

*T*HE CONCEPT OF "THE CHURCH IN THE HOUSE" was introduced and accepted in the early church period. Opposition arose against Paul as he taught the gospel of Jesus Christ in the synagogue. Leaving the synagogue because of persecution, the believing Jews and Gentiles congregated in the homes of other believers for the specific purpose of worship. An account of the church in the house is written in Acts 18:5-11 and can be noted below:

Acts 18:5-11

> 5 And when Silas and Timotheus were come from Macedonia, Paul was pressed in the spirit, and testified to the Jews that Jesus was Christ.

> 6 And when they opposed themselves, and blasphemed, he shook his raiment, and said unto them, Your blood be upon your own heads; I am clean; from henceforth I will go unto the Gentiles.

7 And he departed thence, and entered into a certain man's house, named Justus, one that worshipped God, whose house joined hard to the synagogue.

8 And Crispus, the chief ruler of the synagogue, believed on the Lord with all his house; and many of the Corinthians hearing believed, and were baptized.

9 Then spake the Lord to Paul in the night by a vision, Be not afraid, but speak, and hold not thy peace:

10 For I am with thee, and no man shall set on thee to hurt thee: for I have much people in this city.

11 And he continued there a year and six months, teaching the word of God among them.

The church — *ekklesia* in Greek — is called out; e.g.., a popular meeting place, a religious congregation, a Jewish synagogue; a Christian community of members on earth or saints in heaven, or both; assembly, church (Strong). For this purpose, we are concerned with the term, "Christian congregation," that met in the house.

There are several mentions in scripture of church in the house, twice in the epistles with Priscilla and Aquila, and with two other friends of Paul, Nymphas of Laodacia and Philemon of Colosse. The scriptures follow:

Romans 16:3-5

3 Greet Priscilla and Aquila my helpers in Christ Jesus:

4 Who have for my life laid down their own necks: unto whom not only I give thanks, but also all the churches of the Gentiles.

5 Likewise greet <u>the church that is in their house</u>. Salute my well-beloved Epaenetus, who is the first fruits of Achaia unto Christ.

1 Corinthians 16:19

19 The churches of Asia salute you. Aquila and Priscilla salute you much in the Lord, with <u>the church that is in their house</u>.

Colossians 4:15

15 Salute the brethren which are in Laodicea, and Nymphas, and <u>the church which is in his house</u>.

Philemon 1:1-3

1 Paul, a prisoner of Jesus Christ, and Timothy our brother, unto Philemon our dearly beloved, and fellow labourer,

2 And to our beloved Apphia, and Archippus our fellow soldier, and to <u>the church in thy house</u>:

3 Grace to you, and peace, from God our Father and the Lord Jesus Christ.

Philemon was a Christian friend of Paul who lived in Colosse. He was the master of the runaway slave, Onesimus, who was begotten by Paul (***The Lion Encyclopedia of the Bible***). Tradition says his wife was Apphia and Archippus was his son, the pastor of <u>the church in the home</u> of Philemon (Dake). While it is not spelled out, it is believed that Gaius (3 John Epistle) shared pastoral responsibilities, possibly in Pergamum (Eerdman).

As did the others, Nymphas of Laodacia was, Eerdman states, "One of those who opened their homes to the local Christian groups long before there were church buildings. He further states that the whole church is deeply in debt to them all" (Eerdman).

When I was a little girl, the missionaries of our local church practiced the concept of the church in the house, and even today, certain evangelists hold meetings in the home for the homebound and the unchurched. Before the inception of this ministry, I exercised the same concept. I do it now to confirm the sheep and lambs in the faith and to maintain stability and foster growth.

The church in the house flourished in six instances through New Birth House of Prayer for all People. At the onset of the ministry, January 3, 1980, when the Lord proclaimed, "Out of Egypt I call my son" and commanded me to "Plant four months," I immediately endeavored to obey, as I understood. I planted a garden of vegetables in our backyard as I hid the Word in my heart and invited family and friends to Bible study sessions in our home. My children were with me all the time. After faithfully worshipping there regularly every week for fifteen months, He commissioned me in a vision to "Feed the flock" (Acts 20:28).

When the flock outgrew our living room in 1982, the unknown deep-seated concern of my husband surfaced. It was he who suggested, "You need to start looking for a bigger place." Prayerfully, I agreed. Together, we began searching. God gave us favor with a local Baptist minister (Dr. Jimmy Staten) who had an old, dilapidated building with no windows, no electricity, no plumbing or water, and doors hanging off the hinges. Do I need to tell you that at my first sight of it, I thought, "No way!" However, my husband had the insight that the building could be renovated. My father agreed. We thanked the minister for making the building available to us.

Fifteen years later, Erica, to whom I had given spiritual birth and mothered in the Lord since pre-school days, married and moved with her husband, Al, my spiritual son, and their children to <u>Jacksonville, Florida</u> – that was in August 1995. They chose to remain with the ministry. To that effect, a <u>church in the house</u> was established in their home. At that point in time, we met regularly and continued until the Lord deemed otherwise.

Between the onset of this ministry and the inauguration of the Jacksonville mission in 1995, a church was established in 1989 by Bishop Samuel McCormick in <u>Pompano Beach, Florida.</u>

In 1993, ongoing missionary work continued in <u>Deerfield Beach, Florida</u>, with the work spreading in 1994 to <u>Albany, Georgia</u>; in 1997, to <u>Orlando, Florida</u>; and in 1998, to <u>Fernandina Beach, Florida</u>. The following ministers and families assisted with the work in these locations: Ministers Edwena and Pete Bowles (both deceased); Evangelist Deborah M. Bailey and husband Eric Bailey and their daughters, Danielle and Taylor; Minister James Jackson and Verna "Jackie" Thomas; Al and Erica Mitchell and their children, Marcee and Terique; Cecil and Kim McSwain, Jabari, Jacque and Jada; and Gloria and Bernice Hendrix. Like Jacksonville, most of the missions were started with a person who relocated to these cities, thus becoming first fruit of the New Birth House of Prayer for All People.

In practicality, since establishment of this ministry, I have found the <u>church in the house</u> to be vital to the sheep for confirming them in the faith, preserving them and inducing ministry growth. These young ministries were fulfilling a spiritual need in their locations. Since finances are not always available for the purchase and/or rental of property, I have also found <u>the</u>

church in the house to be the answer. Because of its effectiveness, I highly recommend it.

ELECT LADIES
IN THE BIBLE
(OLD TESTAMENT)

CHAPTER **8**

Elect Ladies as Faith Sheroes

*T*HE CONTRIBUTIONS OF TWO OF THE ELECT
WOMEN, Jochebed (Jewish) in Moses' deliverance,
and Rahab (Gentile) in Israel's conquering of Jericho, were so
outstanding and distinct that the Holy Ghost inspired writings
about them in both the Old Testament and the New Testament.
Because they made biblical headlines, I believe their experiences became "the talk of the town in every generation." Today,
they are listed among the faith heroes in Hebrews, Chapter 11,
with such notables as Abraham, Sarah, Isaac, and Jacob.

Summarily, the scriptures say, "By faith Moses when he
was born was hid three months by his parents (Jochebed and
Amram) because they saw he was a proper child, and they were
not afraid of the king's commandment" (Hebrews 11:23).

Subsequently, by faith, the harlot, Rahab, perished not with
them that believed not when she had received the spies with
peace (Hebrews 11:31). Although a harlot, Rahab's name is
given as the mother of Boaz in Matthew's list of Jesus' ances-
tors (*The Lion Encyclopedia of the Bible*, Joshua 2:1; Matthew
1:5; James 2:25)

CHAPTER 9

Elect Ladies Involved in Moses' Deliverance

*F*OR 430 YEARS THE PEOPLE OF JACOB remained in Egypt. During that time, they had grown into a nation – the nation of Israel. The Egyptians, now ruled by a less friendly dynasty of kings, began to see these people as a threat. They tightened their control, forcing the Israelites to work as slaves in brickfields (Exodus 12:40-41).

To reduce their growing numbers, the king made a decree to destroy all male children! This was an attempt of Satan to destroy all males of Israel so the Messiah could not come to bruise his head. The future of Israel as a nation and the unborn deliverer's life were at stake. The plan of redemption was also threatened but, in the nick of time, God intervened in the affairs of Israel so that He might fulfill His promise to Abraham: *In thee shall all families of the earth be blessed* (Genesis 12:3).

To execute His plan of redemption, God chose certain women from among the Jews and Gentiles, each with a distinct duty: He chose Shiphrah and Puah, two Hebrew midwives, and Jochebed, the daughter of Levi and wife of Amram, to be the mother of Moses. Miriam, their daughter, was chosen to be Moses' older sister, and believe it or not, God chose Thermuthis, the daughter of Pharaoh, Israel's staunch enemy and oppressor who reigned at that time, to be Moses' patroness.

Although these ladies are from different nationalities and circumstances, God knew they would make a powerful agency and — hallelujah! — His plan was executed.

Moses was saved! To take a look at the performance of each person, let us read the story as presented in Exodus 1:15-22; 2:1-10 in the Amplified Bible.

Exodus 1:15-22

> 15 Then the king of Egypt said to the Hebrew midwives, of whom one was named Shiphrah and the other Puah,

> 16 When you act as midwives to the Hebrew women and see them on the birthstool, if it is a son, you shall kill him; but if it is a daughter, she shall live.

> 17 But the midwives feared God and did not do as the king of Egypt commanded, but let the male babies live.

> 18 So the king of Egypt called for the midwives and said to them, Why have you done this thing and allowed the male children to live?

> 19 The midwives answered Pharaoh, Because the Hebrew women are not like the Egyptian women; they are vigorous and quickly delivered; their babies are born before the midwife comes to them.

20 So God dealt well with the midwives and the people multiplied and became very strong.

21 And because the midwives revered *and* feared God, He made them households [of their own].

22 Then Pharaoh charged all his people, saying, Every son born [to the Hebrews] you shall cast into the river [Nile], but every daughter you shall allow to live.

Exodus 2:1-10

1 Now [Amram] a man of the house of Levi [the priestly tribe] went and took as his wife [Jochebed] a daughter of Levi (Exo. 6:18,20; Num. 26:59).

2 And the woman became pregnant and bore a son; and when she saw that he was [exceedingly] beautiful, she hid him three months (Acts 7:20; Heb. 11:23).

3 And when she could no longer hide him, she took for him an ark *or* basket made of bulrushes *or* papyrus [making it watertight by] daubing it with bitumen and pitch. Then she put the child in it and laid it among the rushes by the brink of the river [Nile].

4 And his sister [Miriam] stood some distance away to [a]learn what would be done to him.

5 Now the daughter of Pharaoh came down to bathe at the river, and her maidens walked along the bank; she saw the ark among the rushes and sent her maid to fetch it.

6 When she opened it, she saw the child; and behold, the baby cried. And she took pity on him and said, This is one of the Hebrews' children!

7 Then his sister said to Pharaoh's daughter, Shall I go and call a nurse of the Hebrew women to nurse the child for you?

8 Pharaoh's daughter said to her, Go. And the girl went and called the child's mother.

9 Then Pharaoh's daughter said to her, Take this child away and nurse it for me, and I will give you your wages. So the woman took the child and nursed it.

10 And the child grew, and she brought him to Pharaoh's daughter and he became her son. And she called him Moses, for she said, Because I drew him out of the water.

This example shows election according to purpose. These ladies, the chosen agents of God — Shiphrah, Puah, Jochebed, Miriam, the youngest, and Thermuthis, daughter of Pharaoh — defied the command of the king of Egypt. They were providentially used by God to preserve baby Moses, thus furthering the cause of redemption for both Moses and the nation of Israel, and ultimately the whole world: "the salvation of the righteous is of the Lord: He is their strength in time of trouble. And the Lord shall help them, and deliver them: he shall deliver them from the wicked, and save them, because they trust in him" (Psalm 37: 39-40).

CHAPTER 10

Shiphrah, Puah, Jochebed, Miriam, and Thermuthis (Pharaoh's Daughter)

*S*HIPHRAH AND PUAH, THE HEBREW MIDWIVES, played an important part in the salvation of all the Hebrew boys. The Bible says, "They feared God and did not as the king of Egypt commanded but saved the men children alive...the people multiplied and waxed very mighty" (Exodus 1:17-20).When the midwives were confronted by the king, the answer of their tongue was from the Lord. Therefore, He dealt well with them and he gave them households.

Jochebed (the Lord is glorious), a daughter who was of the house of Levi, married Amram, by whom she bore Moses, Aaron, and Miriam. She built an ark of bulrushes for the salvation of her son, Moses, and was hired by Thermuthis and given wages to care for him.

Miriam (rebellion), the "quick-witted" sister of Moses and Aaron, watched the infant Moses as he lay in the ark of bulrushes. She convinced Thermuthis to hire the baby's mother to nurse him; later, she became a prophetess and leader of women during the Exodus (The Holy Scriptures According to the Masoretic Text). After the Israelites crossed the Red Sea, Miriam led the women in singing and dancing for joy.

Later she and Aaron spake against Moses because of the Ethiopian woman whom he had married and his leadership -which angered God. (Numbers 12: 1-16) For a short time, as punishment, she suffered a terrible skin disease (leprosy), but Moses asked God to heal her. Years later, she died at Kadesh before the Israelites reached Canaan.

Thermuthis, the daughter of Pharaoh (Israel's greatest foe) became the baby's patroness (*The Amplified Bible*). She had compassion for the baby Moses, and said to his mother, "Take this child away and nurse it for me, and I will give you wages." Later he became her son; and she called his name Moses and said, "Because I drew him out of the water".

CHAPTER 11

Rahab the Harlot Helps Israel Conquer Jericho

*A*FTER MOSES DELIVERED THE CHILDREN OF ISRAEL out of Egyptian bondage, his mission assigned by God, is fulfilled, and Joshua assumes command to bring them into the Promised Land. The scenario focuses on them in Shittim, the eastern campsite of Israel before entering Canaan. Facing a very crucial point, Joshua, the leader, strategizes and sends out two men to spy secretly. As the story unfolds, a harlot of Jericho, who lives in a house on the wall, becomes involved. By defying the command of the king of Jericho, she becomes the link to Israel's conquering Jericho.

Her cooperation with the two spies results in the salvation of both her and her father's household and victory for Israel. Joshua 2:1-21 in the Amplified Bible reads:

Joshua 2:1-21

> Joshua son of Nun sent two men secretly from Shittim as scouts, saying, Go, view the land, especially Jericho.

And they went and came to the house of a harlot named Rahab and lodged there.

2 It was told the king of Jericho, Behold, there came men in here tonight of the Israelites to search out the country.

3 And the king of Jericho sent to Rahab, saying, Bring forth the men who have come to you, who entered your house, for they have come to search out the land.

4 But the woman had taken the two men and hidden them. So she said, Yes, two men came to me, but I did not know from where they had come.

5 And at gate closing time, after dark, the men went out. Where they went I do not know. Pursue them quickly, for you will overtake them.

6 But she had brought them up to the roof and hidden them under the stalks of flax which she had laid in order there.

7 So the men pursued them to the Jordan as far as the fords. As soon as the pursuers had gone, the city's gate was shut.

8 Before the two men had lain down, Rahab came up to them on the roof,

9 And she said to the men, I know that the Lord has given you the land and that your terror is fallen upon us and that all the inhabitants of the land faint becauseof you.

10 For we have heard how the Lord dried up the water of the Red Sea for you when you came out of Egypt, and what you did to the two kings of the Amoriteswho

were on the [east] side of the Jordan, Sihon and Og, whom you utterly destroyed.

11 When we heard it, our hearts melted, neither did spirit *or* courage remain any more in any man because of you, for the Lord your God, He is God in heaven above and on earth beneath.

12 Now then, I pray you, swear to me by the Lord, since I have shown youkindness, that you also will show kindness to my father's house, and give me a sure sign,

13 And save alive my father and mother, my brothers and sisters, and all they have, and deliver us from death.

14 And the men said to her, Our lives for yours! If you do not tell this business of ours, then when the Lord gives us the land we will deal kindly and faithfully with you.

15 Then she let them down by a rope through the window, for her house was built into the [town] wall so that she dwelt in the wall.

16 And she said to them, Get to the mountain, lest the pursuers meet you; hide yourselves there three days until the pursuers have returned; and afterward you may go your way.

17 The men said to her, We will be blameless of this oath you have made us swear. [The responsibility is now yours.]

18 Behold, when we come into the land, you shall bind this scarlet cord in the window through which you let us down, and you shall bring your father and mother,

your brothers, and all your father's household into
your house.

19 And if anyone goes out of the doors of your house
into the street, his blood shall be upon his head, and we
will be guiltless; but if a hand is laid upon anyone who
is with you in the house, his blood shall be on our head.

20 But if you tell this business of ours, we shall be guiltless of your oath which you made us swear.

21 And she said, According to your words, so it is. Then
she sent them away and they departed; and she bound
the scarlet cord in the window.

After the wall of Jericho fell flat and Israel had utterly
destroyed all that was in the city, Joshua said, to the two men
who had spied out the land, 'Go into the harlot's house and
bring out the woman and all she has, as you swore to her'. So
the young men, the spies, went in and brought out Rahab... and
all her kindred and sat them outside the camp of Israel. And
they burned the city with fire and all that was in it... and saved
Rahab the harlot with her father's household and all that she
had; and she lives in Israel even to this day, because she hid the
messengers who Joshua sent to spy out Jericho (*The Amplified
Bible*; Joshua 6:21-25)

CHAPTER 12

Elect Ladies in Old Testament Ministry

KEEPING THE DOCUMENTED CHARGE OF GOD was no minor task for the children of Israel. They were known for keeping records, written notes, and written artifacts. This was a reminder that God told each leader to document His writings and teach them to the people. Each leader was reminded to tell of God's commands and to not let them depart from their hearts, minds, and ears. He gave this charge to Israel, to pass down His laws from generation to generation.

Huldah

Known as a prophetess during the 31-year reign of King Josiah, Huldah was a wife, prophetess and an authenticator. She declared written words to be the word of God – Scripture and they came to pass. In the eighteenth year of King Josiah, the book of the law was discovered. The King commanded Hilkiah the priest and Ahikam and Achbor, Shaphan and Asaiah... saying, go ye, inquire of the Lord for me and the people and for all Judah concerning the words of this book that is found: for the wrath of the Lord that is kindled against us, because our fathers have not hearkened unto the words of this book, to do according unto all that which is written concerning us. So, they went unto Huldah. She said unto them Thus saith the Lord God of Israel, Tell the man that sent you to me, Thus saith the Lord, Behold, I will bring evil upon this place, and upon the inhabitants thereof, even all the words of the book which the king of Judah hath read: Because they have forsaken me, and have burned incense unto other gods, that they might provoke me to anger with all the works of their hands; therefore my wrath shall be kindled against this place, and shall not be quenched. But to the king of Judah which sent you to enquire of the Lord, thus shall ye say to him, Thus saith the Lord God of Israel, As touching the words which thou hast heard; Because thine heart was tender, and thou hast humbled thyself before the Lord, when thou heardest what I spake against this place, and against the inhabitants thereof, that they should become a desolation and a curse, and hast rent thy clothes, and wept before me; I also have heard thee, saith the Lord. Behold therefore, I will gather thee unto thy fathers, and thou shall be gathered unto thy grave in peace; and thine eyes shall not see all the evil which I will bring upon this place. And they brought the king word again (2 Kings 22:8-20). The word of the Lord spoken by Prophetess Huldah came to pass.

What an awesome honor! Huldah was married to Shallum who was the "keeper of the wardrobe" (2 Kings 22:14). The scriptures indicate that when Hilkiah, Ahikam, Achbor, Shaphan, and Asaiah came to her home, they did not ask for her husband. It was Huldah they inquired of, and it is clear that there was no embarrassment or disrespect over their inquiring into God's will from a woman. This leads us to believe that their high priest did not have an issue with a woman prophet; therefore, why should we?

The role of a prophet/prophetess is also one of the five-fold ministries, as revealed in Ephesians 4:11-16. It is helpful to explain the role and use of a prophet/prophetess. They are inspired messengers who speak for God, delivering a message that God has ordained him or her to give. Prophets express the will of God in words, and sometimes they use signs to back up what they are saying and to demonstrate God's power behind it. The prophet's primary responsibility is to bring about restoration, balance and order as well as to speak out against injustice, abuse and blatant unfairness in the church, the marketplace and government. The prophet is a warrior, a watchman, and a gatekeeper and is constantly in a state of readiness to do battle in the heavens. Prophets and prophetesses are warriors, not competitors, and the spirit of competition does not exist in the life of a prophet or prophetess.

Our role as leaders, judges, pastors, and overseers is not to be competitive or to prove to individuals that we are called by God. Huldah was one whose works and lifestyle spoke for themselves, and it was apparent that her advice was valuable to the men of the court and to King Josiah. My aim through this journey is to encourage women, using God's written words, to move into your called position and destiny as He has so divinely instructed you.

Deborah

The office of prophet in the Old Testament was not limited to men; there were a few other women, in addition to Huldah, who were called to be prophetesses, God's spokespersons, as were the prophets. Miriam (ca. 1400 B.C.) (Exodus 15:20) was the first prophetess to the nation of Israel, then Deborah (Judges 4:3-7), Isaiah's wife, was also a prophetess (725 B.C.) (Isaiah 8:3). There were female prophets in the early New Testament times; we see this with Philip, "Now this man had four virgin daughters who were prophetesses" (Acts 21:9).

Judges 4:4-8

[4] And Deborah, a prophetess, the wife of Lapidoth, she judged Israel at that time.

[5] And she dwelt under the palm tree of Deborah between Ramah and Bethel in mount Ephraim: and the children of Israel came up to her for judgment.

[6] And she sent and called Barak the son of Abinoam out of Kedeshnaphtali, and said unto him, Hath not the LORD God of Israel commanded, saying, Go and draw toward mount Tabor, and take with thee ten thousand men of the children of Naphtali and of the children of Zebulun?

[7] And I will draw unto thee to the river Kishon Sisera, the captain of Jabin's army, with his chariots and his multitude; and I will deliver him into thine hand.

[8] And Barak said unto her, If thou wilt go with me, then I will go: but if thou wilt not go with me, then I will not go.

Judges (leaders) were a select group of individuals who ruled Israel. While they performed most judicial duties, the office of judges was separate from the office of king. Deborah was a prophetess and judge in the time of the Judges; she was unique among the women and men of the Bible's history – in that she was a prophetess, a judge, a military leader and spouse, all in one. Like Moses and Samuel, among the Israelites, Deborah was authentic and exemplified powerful roles of authority and responsibility. Wow!

Esther (The book of Esther)

Using ordinary people for extraordinary work was no minimal charge for God. Esther, the first recorded beauty queen, was God's unlikely candidate for delivering His people from destruction. This wonderful story, as shared in Old Testament scriptures, the book of Esther, reveals the delicate position in which she was placed. When reading the story of Esther, we can see she was skilled in diplomacy and reared for such a task. The story of Esther is an illustration of how God can use an orphan by allowing her to go through a series of tests. She was a participant in the first-recorded beauty pageant. Through the grace and favor of God, Esther was the king's choice and made queen of Persia, the largest kingdom in the world at that time. We can clearly see that Esther was certainly positioned to be a leader destined to save God's people. Though a foreigner and having been a captive, Esther was captive and chosen by God to deliver His people. Esther's name means "hidden," appropriate for such a time. Her true identity and heritage were hidden until the appropriate time God wanted to deliver His people. Several leadership roles and positions demonstrate how God has used women to lead, judge, shepherd, and/or nurture His people.

CHAPTER 13

Elect Ladies in New Testament Ministry

*I*N THE DISCUSSION OF THE DOCTRINE OF ELECTION, we were informed earlier by Dake that all Christians are the elect of God, even as are Christ, Israel, and angels. Anyone chosen of God, are called to become God's elect or chosen ones and can be if they will choose God.

Scofield also added that election is the sovereign act of God in grace, whereby certain elect persons are chosen from among mankind for Himself or for distinctive service for Him. Clearly, this was exemplified in those persons chosen by God to partake in the deliverance of Moses and of the nation of Israel in pursuance of the Promised Land.

With this valuable information imparted, let us consider the contributions of elect ladies of the New Testament before during the infancy, public ministry and post ministry of Jesus. But first, let's reflect on the story of Elisabeth; these are my observations in truth and practicality of them.

Elisabeth, Mary's cousin and mother of John the Baptist – the forerunner of Jesus
Luke 1:13, 36-45

[13] But the angel said unto him, Fear not, Zacharias: for thy prayer is heard; and thy wife Elisabeth shall bear thee a son, and thou shalt call his name John.

[36] And, behold, thy cousin Elisabeth, she hath also conceived a son in her old age: and this is the sixth month with her, who was called barren.

[37] For with God nothing shall be impossible.

[38] And Mary said, Behold the handmaid of the Lord; be it unto me according to thy word. And the angel departed from her.

[39] And Mary arose in those days, and went into the hill country with haste, into a city of Juda;

[40] And entered into the house of Zacharias, and saluted Elisabeth.

[41] And it came to pass, that, when Elisabeth heard the salutation of Mary, the babe leaped in her womb; and Elisabeth was filled with the Holy Ghost:

[42] And she spake out with a loud voice, and said, Blessed art thou among women, and blessed is the fruit of thy womb.

[43] And whence is this to me, that the mother of my Lord should come to me?

⁴⁴ For, lo, as soon as the voice of thy salutation sounded in mine ears, the babe leaped in my womb for joy.

⁴⁵ And blessed is she that believed: for there shall be a performance of those things which were told her from the Lord.

For with God nothing shall be impossible (Luke 1:37). Elisabeth and Mary were empowered by God to bare sons and given their names. Both miraculously conceived sons to promote the beginning of Christianity.

Infancy of Jesus
Mary the Mother of God: The Biological Nurturer

In the beginning was the Word, and the Word was with God, and the Word was God (John 1:1)

And the Word was made flesh, and dwelt among us, (and we beheld his glory, the glory as of the only begotten of the Father,) full of grace and truth (John 1:14)

During Jesus' infancy, there were some outstanding women who were instrumental in the life of Christ. God's selection of those whom He chooses for specific roles is by His design, not ours. His selection of Mary is notable of all the women in her village, making Mary quite special. He describes her as "highly favored" (Luke 1:28).

The angel further tells Mary that she will be the mother of Jesus Christ (Luke 1:31). Instead of rebutting and openly refusing, she offers a poem of praise. (Luke 1:46-55). Mary gave birth (Luke 2:5-7) and thought about the wonderful things said about Jesus (Luke 2:19). She was blessed by Elizabeth (Luke 1:42). It is believed that Mary did not understand but treasured the sayings about Jesus.

God's design is nothing like ours. In the Old Testament scriptures, we clearly see how God used women to spiritually and physically nurture, lead, judge and instruct His people. The New Testament shows a more intimate service by Mary, who physically carried Jesus in the womb, and nurtured His life from infancy to adulthood. In addition, Anna was chosen by God to tell others that the Savior of the world had been born.

Anna the Proclaimer

At the time of the birth of Christ, Anna was a prophetess who was at the Temple when the Messiah was brought there as an infant. Anna, the prophetess, was the daughter of Phanuel of the tribe of Asher. She was of a great age and lived with her husband seven years, and she was a widow of about fourscore and four (84) years, who departed not from the temple, but served God with fasting and prayers night and day. God used her to proclaim [announce] that Jesus was the Redeemer, the promised Messiah. (Luke 2:36-38)

Jesus' Public Ministry
The Samaritan Woman Evangelist

During Jesus' public ministry the Samaritan woman at the well was converted and chosen to carry the message to others about salvation through Jesus Christ. Many in Samaria were converted as a result of her evangelism. (John 4:5-42). Here in practicality, she was performing as an evangelist.

Jesus' Post Resurrection Ministry

Through the post resurrection ministry of Jesus, we have another example of evangelism, Mary Magdelene, and the other Mary and some other women were given a charge by Jesus to give to the Disciples. He said to them, "Go tell the

Disciples and Peter to meet Him in Galilee"(Matt. 28, Mark 16, Luke 24 and John 20)

Other women such as Priscilla, Junia and the elect lady of the 2 Epistle of John, were ministers who were instrumental in developing apostolic leaders and nurturing disciples. What an awesome God!

Special note: God trusted a woman to carry Jesus, the Word, in her womb, as well as to train and instruct Him throughout His young life and adulthood. Therefore, it follows that He would trust other women of faith to preach and teach the Gospel of Jesus Christ.

CHAPTER 14

Priscilla

*V*ENTURE NOW WITH ME TO WOMEN MINISTERS WHO WERE INSTRUMENTAL IN ADVANCING THE KINGDOM OF GOD, where we find Priscilla and Junia; and the elect lady as previously defined in chapter 1. They were women of eminence in the first century church who were dutiful disciples in the work of God and in the walk of truth. In exchanging ideas about them, we will begin with Priscilla.

Priscilla's name is mentioned six times in the New Testament, once as Prisca (2 Tim 4;19), but always as Priscilla with her Jewish husband, Aquila, in business and in ministry. She is mentioned three times in the book of (Acts 18:2,18, 26) and once in the epistles of (Romans 16:3); and (1 Corinthians 16:19). Indications are that they were one flesh (Genesis 2:24; Matthew 19:5-6) and one spirit (1 Corinthians 6:17). It is my opinion from scripture observation, they were the first model husband and wife ministry team in the New Testament. Married Christians can benefit largely from their example of unity in the faith. Their home was in Rome, Italy, but they were forced to leave Italy when the Emperor Claudius expelled the Jews from Rome in A.D. 48. Like Paul, they were tentmakers.

And, for a time, Paul stayed and worked with them in Corinth. When Paul traveled to Ephesus, Priscilla and her husband went with him. Later, they moved back to Rome. In both places, Christians met in their homes (Romans 16:3-5; 1 Corinthians 16:19); *The Lion Encyclopedia of the Bible*)

Priscilla in the Ministry of Helps

Priscilla's ministries of the New Testament are seen as she operates in the ministry of helps and in the ministry of the teacher with Aquila.

"And God hath set some in the church, first apostles; secondarily, prophets; thirdly teachers, after that miracles, then, gifts of healing, helps..." (1 Corinthians 12:28).

First, let us talk about the ministry of helps. In Greek, the word helps is "antilepsis," which signifies a support, help; a succorer, an aid – referring to every kind of help God sets in the church. It cannot be limited to the work of deacons and deaconesses, as some teach; for there were other helps besides these (Romans 16:3, 9; 1 Corinthians 16:15-16; 2 Corinthians 1:11, 24). It does not refer to persons only but also to the various spiritual gifts, which endow men with power to help (Dake).

In context, Priscilla is active with her husband in the ministry of helps; they are acknowledged as such by the Apostle Paul. In a letter to the Roman Christians, he says, "Greet Priscilla and Aquila, my helpers (companion, co-laborers) in Christ Jesus" (Romans 16:3; Vine). In addition, *Eerdman's Concise Handbook of the Bible* states that "Everywhere this hospitable pair went they were a great support to young churches."

Priscilla, with her husband, followed in the same pursuit with Paul, as did John Mark with Barnabas and Saul. The scripture says, they had John Mark as their minister (Acts 13:5)

As it was then, so it is now; the ministry of helps is a much-needed ministry in the church. Busy, dedicated, and righteous leaders can use such helps to relieve them of the overload that often exists. Besides, this ministry can be useful in edifying the body, as well.

Priscilla as a Teacher

"And He gave some teachers. . . ." (Ephesians 4:11).

The New Thayer's Greek-English Lexicon of the New Testament says, "A teacher in the New Testament is one who teaches the things of God and the duties of man; those who in religious assemblies of Christians undertook the work of teaching with the special assistance of Holy Ghost; one who is fitted to teach or thinks himself so." Also, a teacher is one who gives instruction and trains (Vines).

In Acts 18:24-26 (Scofield), Priscilla and her husband functioned as teachers. Read the scripture which follows:

Acts 18:24-26

24 And a certain Jew named Apollos, born at Alexandria, an eloquent man, and mighty in the scriptures, came to Ephesus.

25 This man was instructed in the way of the Lord; and being fervent in thespirit, he spake and taught diligently the things of the Lord, knowing only the baptism of John.

26 And he began to speak boldly in the synagogue: whom when Aquila and Priscilla had heard, they took him unto them, and expounded unto him the way of God more perfectly.

Eerdman's says, "Thanks to Aquila and Priscilla this eloquent Alexandrian (Apollos) became a man of great influence in the Corinthian Church" as stated below in Acts 18:27-28:

Acts 18:27-28

27 And when he was disposed to pass into Achaia, the brethren wrote, exhorting the disciples to receive him: who, when he was come, helped them much which had believed through grace:

28 For he mightily convinced the Jews, and that publicly, shewing by the scriptures that Jesus was Christ.

Priscilla, with her husband, exemplified good qualities of teachers sent from God; they recognized the need and filled it as God worked through them, perfecting the saints for the work of the ministry (Ephesians 4:12).

Besides functioning in the ministries of helps and teaching, scripture associates Priscilla with the church in the house discussed in chapter 7.

I conclude finally, as workers together, Aquila and Priscilla, male and female, husband and wife, and equals in ministry, were used by God to demonstrate that He is no respecter of persons, but in every nation, he that feareth Him and worketh righteousness is acceptable with Him (Acts 10:34-35). In addition, Paul states there is neither Jew nor Greek, there is neither bond nor free; there is neither male nor female: "for ye are all one in Christ Jesus" (Galatians 3:28). So Priscilla and Aquila exemplified equality in Christ.

CHAPTER 15

Junia, the Apostle

THE APOSTLE IS A PIONEER WHO IS DESTINED to build or rebuild in places of desolation and ruin. Apostles bring revelatory teaching to the body of Christ. The apostle creates order in a new work or in an existing work that is dealing with a spirit of chaos. As builders and founders, apostles have an anointing to identify, mentor, and mature leaders. They are not fearful of hard work and will not shy away from secular work. Their responsibilities include evangelizing, setting up and organizing churches, handling problems that arise, ordaining elders for each church, and generally coordinating, supervising and serving various congregations.

Dianne McDonnell of Freedom Ministry provides an in-depth look at the meaning of the name, Junia; the significance of her gender; and her role in ministry, according to Greek studies. She indicates that in Thayer's Greek definition, Junia is a common Latin female name meaning "youthful." In Paul's writing, we find that she, along with Andronicus, were mentioned as kinsman; it is here that we are provided a glimpse of her works and the role she plays as an apostle.

Since Paul mentions Junia as a kinsman, he would know her best as he praised both Andronicus and her as outstanding among the apostles. Just as Paul considered himself to be an apostle, it is in Romans 16:7 that we are told both were part of the group called apostles; they were apostles and were setting an outstanding example in the gospel work.

McDonnell further states in her writings that "Junia was a very common Latin female name, and we have no record of any Roman male bearing the name Junia." But medieval copyists began copying the name with an "s" to hide Junia's sex, not knowing that the name Junia "did not exist in antiquity." Junia was given this highest spiritual gift along with her husband Andronicus, indicating that women can also be given the calling (spiritual gift) of serving God as prophets, teachers, or embodying any of the other spiritual gifts.

We read in the scriptures, there is no indication that any gift is limited to males only. McDonnell, along with countless others, believed that both men and women are to work together using whatever talents, abilities and spiritual gifts they have been given by God to serve, in a servant manner, the people of God.

Romans 16:7

7 Salute Andronicus and Junia, my kinsmen, and my fellow-prisoners, who are of note among the apostles, who also were in Christ before me.

Accomplishing His Purpose as an ELECT LADY IN MINISTRY NOW

All things work together for good for them that love the Lord and are called according to his purpose. Romans 8:28

The Lord is GOOD! Jesus gets all the praise. I am thankful that God has chosen me to do His work. God told me to go, and I went. Jesus said, But ye shall receive power, after that the Holy Ghost is come upon you: and ye shall be <u>witnesses</u> unto me both in Jerusalem, and in all Judea, and in Samaria, and unto the uttermost part of the earth. (Acts 1:8)

<u>**"Assemble All My People,"**</u> He said to me in April 1981.

On August 9, 1987, the LORD showed me the name, ALBUQUERQUE. I will share more about that vision a little further down.

"I've Got to Do What I Gotta Do When Nobody Else Will Do." The harvest is truly ripe, and I must go and do my share! In April 2014, God said I have set before you AN OPEN

DOOR and told me to "AFFIX ASSESS to WESTCOAST." Subsequently he said, "CONNECT WITH BISHOP PORTER."

With them the open door extended to minister and fellowship with the APACHES and the NAVAJOS, NATIVE PEOPLE OF AMERICA. In July of 2017, thirty years after the Lord showed me Albuquerque, New Mexico, more of the commission to assemble all my people was fulfilled when God told me to "connect with" Bishop Porter and I thank God.

I had the opportunity to travel to Albuquerque, New Mexico with Henry L. Porter Evangelist Association (HLPEA). That truly was my OPEN DOOR.

God blessed us to minister in: MALAYSIA, SOUTHEAST ASIA (Petaling Jaya and Puchong) GHANA, WEST AFRICA (Accra, Elmina, Komenda, Sekondi-Takoradi) SOUTH AFRICA (Cape Town, and four or five of its townships) once again, in association with Henry L. Porter Evangelistic Association (HLPEA).

Throughout my travels, some of the airports were noticeably large, especially when we had a layover in EUROPE — PARIS, FRANCE! I made sacrifices to go! I wish you could be with me in the harvest of the souls.

Yes, I have reached 80 years of age, and GOD IS USING ME and, I thank God for those who helped me. Jesus said, "Be ye ready also: for the Son of man cometh at an hour when ye think not."

Oh, while in South Africa, I discovered that my record "DO WHATCHA GOTTA DO" is on iTunes. Download it online! Just search my name, Queen McCormick!

Conclusion

*F*ROM ANOTHER PERSPECTIVE OF ELECTION, the experiences that have been discussed in this study, from the beginning to the end (Old Testament – New Testament) and modern day, revealed elect ladies were chosen by God to perform distinctive services and/or specific vocations unto Him relative to the deliverance and preservation of His people, serving among both Jews and Gentiles. Their roles varied from helpers to specific vocations for God. In His sovereignty, God has shown that He is no respecter of persons and that He uses His creation when, where, and how He desires to accomplish His purpose.

My Prayer

Father, I thank You for the opportunity
to glorify You through this work.
I pray that it will destroy doubt, ignorance and
fear among those whom You have chosen
to be helpers and leaders for the advancement of your kingdom.

May there be wider acceptance of women in ministry
that the reader of this work would be encouraged
and the sinner may be won to You, and the saints preserved
until the day of Jesus' return.

Amen.

Works Cited

The Amplified Bible, Zondervan Bible Publisher, Grand Rapids, Michigan, 1987.

Dake, Fenis Jennings, *Dake's Annotated Reference Bible,* Lawrenceville, Georgia, Dake Bible Sales, Inc., 1963.

Eerdman, William B., *Eerdman's Concise Bible Handbook,* William E. Eerdman Publishing, World Wide Publishers, Minneapolis, Minnesota, 1973.

Hayford, Jack W., *God's Daughter and God's Work*, Thomas Nelson Publishers, Nashville, Tennessee, 1994.

The Holy Scriptures According to the Masoretic Text, Delair Publishing, Melrose Park, Illinois, 1988.

The Lion Encyclopedia of the Bible, Reader's Digest, Lion Publishing, 1998.

McCormick, Queen Esther W., *Doctoral Research Project*, "I Must Work the Works of Him That Sent Me While it is Day," New Birth House of Prayer for all People, Fort Lauderdale, Florida, 1995.

Merriam-Webster's Dictionary, Merriam-Webster Incorporated, Springfield, Massachusetts, U.S.A., 1994.

Merrill, Daryl, *God's Order for the Local Church*, A Doctoral Dissertation.

Morris, William, *The American Heritage Dictionary,* Houghton-Mifflin Company, Boston, Massachusetts, 1981.

Scofield, C.I., *The New Scofield Reference Bible,* Oxford Press, New York, 1967.

Strong, James, *The New Strong's Exhaustive Concordance of the Bible,* Thomas Nelson Publishers, Nashville, Tennessee, 1995.

Thayer, J.H., *The New Thayer's Greek-English Lexicon of the New Testament,* Hendrickson Publishers, Peabody, Massachusetts, 1981.

Travis, Charles, *Discover Your Gifts,* Logos Publishing, Jacksonville, Florida, 1995.

Vine, W.E., *Vine's Expository Dictionary of Biblical Words,* Thomas Nelson Publishers, Nashville, Tennessee, 1985.

References

McDonnell, D. Junia The Apostle. Freedom Ministry. *http:// www.churchofgoddfw.com/monthly/junia.shtml*

Swidler, Leonard. (1976). Women in Judaism: The Status of Women in Formative Judaism. Metuchen: The Scarecrow Press

Witherington, Ben, III. (1984). Women in the Ministry of Jesus: Cambridge: Cambridge University Press.

About the Author

For such a time as this, she was born and named before birth by the angel of the Lord, who appeared to her grandmother while she was yet in her mother's womb. "Name her Queen Esther," and so it was done by her parents.

Dr. Queen Esther Williams McCormick, devoted wife of 50 years to the late Bishop Samuel Lee McCormick, is the proud mother of six daughters, grandmother of twelve and great-grandmother of nine. She is the daughter of the late Bishop Solomon Williams, Sr. and the late Reverend Minnie Lee Williams. Growing up she was always active in her family, church and school. She functioned as a chorister throughout Elementary and senior High School. Before graduating from high school Queen became a care giver for her siblings. She served as an usher, a choir member, Sunday school secretary, state youth superintendent, member of the home and prison outreach ministry, and in other capacities in the church. While in ecumenical services under the auspices of chief overseer Bishop M.F. L. Keith, and her local pastor, Elder Rosa L. Hardimon-Thomas both of the Keith Dominion House of God Which is the Church of the Living God, Pillar and Ground of the Truth Church in the mid-1940s through 1980.

A 1960 graduate of Dillard High School in Fort Lauderdale, Florida, Queen received a diploma from Brown Institute of Broadcasting in 1975; a bachelor's degree in theology from International Seminary, Plymouth, Florida, in June 1986; an honorary doctorate of divinity from Undenominational Bible Institute of James City, North Carolina in 1992; a master of biblical studies from Logos Graduate School in Jacksonville, Florida in 1993; and a doctorate of ministry from Logos Graduate School in Jacksonville, Florida, 1996. In addition to continuing her education, she was an active participant in political and civic organizations, including but not limited to the PTA at her children's school, the Urban League, Kiwanis, OIC, and Operation Big Vote. In 1971, she ran for school board member-at-large. She served as President of CUSH (Churches United to Stop HIV) for two years.

In 1974, Dr. McCormick began her radio ministry at WEXY as a gospel newscaster. On April 1, 1978, she broaden her horizon and became a hostess of her own show **Gospel Music Sounds** (incorporating the music, word, and prayer). This move became an extensive career as a radio evangelist. For more than forty years, Dr. McCormick gave radio audiences words of inspiration on WEXY, WRBD, WAVS in Fort Lauderdale, Florida and WIYD in Palatka, FL. She was also a presenter at WGEN television station in Miami, Florida an adjunct professor at International Seminary in Plymouth, Florida and New Birth Bible Institution in Ft Lauderdale. In addition to being the host of "Feed the Flock" radio ministry, she is founder and president of Compassionate Hearts and Serving Hands, a non-profit organization that offers intervention and prevention services for high-risk families residing in Broward County.

She has extended the outreach ministry to include Temporary Housing for people in need; Juveniles Achieving Goals (Project JAG); Women of Potency (WOP), HIV testing site 2001-2020, Project Aid Care Case Management (PAC) Waiver, Condom Distribution, Gateway Community Outreach, and collaborated with the Dept. Of Corrections Volunteer program. Dr. McCormick is also founder of Seed Time Academy and Higher Learning, Queen McCormick's Ministries, Spring Connection, and Elect Lady Conference. She is an ordained Bishop and co-founder, with her late husband and daughters, of New Birth House of Prayer for all People Ministries. She is co-founder, along with her late husband, Bishop Samuel McCormick, of South Florida Quartet Convention.

At thirty-seven years of age, Dr. McCormick answered a series of visions and audible instructions from God to "Feed the Flock" and to "Assemble all My People." She entered the ministry full-time, and found the time to author a book, *The Elect Lady in Ministry* and a background singer with the nationally known Williams Sisters, and their families. After having labored in the ministry for over sixty years, Dr. McCormick's vision for the ministry remains to advance the kingdom of God through active ecumenical teaching and serving. Committed to the cause, this mighty woman of God continues to win souls for the Body of Christ and to "advance the Kingdom of God through Kingdom Works."

Photos #1 & #2 (Church in the House, 1982)
Photo #3 (1st Church Building in 1982 with the McCormick Sisters singing)
Photos #4-#8 (2nd Church Building 1985-1992)

Photo #9 (Dr. McCormick's graduation)   Photo #10 (2nd Church Building
1985-1992)   Photo #11 (Ground Breaking of New/Current Facility, 1992)
Photo #12-#16 (Building progress through the completion)

Photo #17 (Building progress through the completion)
Photo #18 (Recording CD of Dr. McCormick, 2007)
Photos #19-#20 (McCormick Family, 2009)
Photo #21 (Dr. McCormick in Albany, GA, 2009)
Photo #22 (Youth Shut-in, 2010)

NBHOP Men presenting red roses to Pastor McCormick

Happy 78th Birthday
April 6, 2019

Apostle Queen McCormick in Ghana with King

Photos #23-25 (NBHOP, 2013)   Photos #25, #27, #28 (Dr. McCormick, international ministry with HLPEA, 2017-2019)   Photo #29 (Dr. McCormick in Ghana, Africa - international ministry with HLPEA, 2019)
Photo #30 (Dr. McCormick in Ghana, Africa with King, 2019)

CPSIA information can be obtained
at www.ICGtesting.com
Printed in the USA
BVHW050825080322
630893BV00022B/656